A Little Book of
SLIME

A FIREFLY BOOK

Published by Firefly Books Ltd. 2012

First printing

Publisher Cataloging-in-Publication Data (U.S.)

A CIP record of this book is available from Library of Congress

Library and Archives Canada Cataloging in Publication

A CIP record of this book is available from Library and Archives Canada

Published in the United States by
Firefly Books (U.S.) Inc.
P.O. Box 1338, Ellicott Station
Buffalo, New York 14205

Published in Canada by
Firefly Books Ltd.
66 Leek Crescent
Richmond Hill, Ontario L4B 1H1

Printed China

Conceived, edited, and designed by:
Marshall Editions
The Old Brewery
6 Blundell Street
London N7 9BH, UK

Publisher: James Ashton-Tyler
Managing editor: Miranda Smith
Project editor: Elise See Tai
Design: Ali Scrivens
Production: Nikki Ingram
Picture research: Veneta Bullen

A Little Book of
SLIME

Clint Twist

FIREFLY BOOKS

Contents

The lattice stinkhorn is a fungus that produces a sticky slime from which new lattice stinkhorns can grow!

What Is Slime?

It looks and feels slimy. But what is it? Slime is a sticky, semi-liquid substance, such as saliva and frogspawn, that is produced by a living **organism**. Chemically speaking, slime consists of water, along with other ingredients that give slime its peculiar character.

Jelly fungus, see page 68

Mucus

The most common form of slime is mucus, which animals use to keep their bodies moist.

Phlegm, see page 61

In the case of **amphibians**, slugs, and snails, mucus covers the outside of their bodies, as well as parts of their insides. With other animals, such as mammals, birds, and reptiles, mucus is found inside their bodies, for example, on the lining of the lungs. Apart from water, the other main ingredients of mucus are mucins (chemicals that thicken water).

Independent slime

Some slime appears to exist without an organism to produce it. That is because the organisms are the slime. Certain types of **bacteria** and microscopic plants that live in water can be so packed together that they make the water slimy.

Frogspawn, see page 28

Special purpose slime

Slime often contains substances that make it special. The plant mucus is mucilage, and the mucilage produced by the sundew plant contains sugar that makes it extra sticky. The slime produced by the poison arrow frog provides double protection—the slime keeps it moist, and powerful poisons deter other animals from eating the frog. The velvet worm squirts a slime that contains gluelike chemicals, which then harden.

Spare a thought for slime

Slime may look and feel disgusting, but it is essential to plants, animals, and many other organisms—including ourselves. The next time you encounter some slime, try to remember that it is more than just a blob of gunk.

Slime-ometer ratings

Each slimy example in this book has been given a slime-ometer rating between 1 and 10, and is scored according to overall sliminess, unpleasantness, and how dangerous it is—the higher the rating, the worse the slime!

Red tide, see page 15

Saliva, see page 59

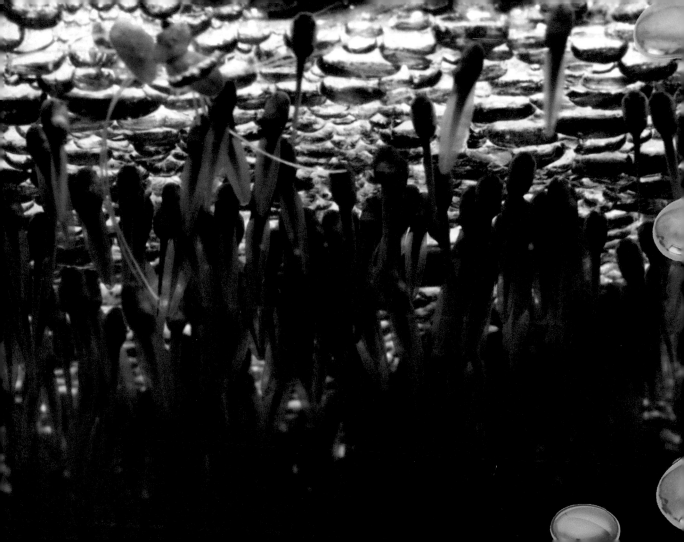

Slimy Stuff in Water

Slime and water do not mix, but that is the beauty of slime. Eventually, the slime will dissolve, but in the meantime, it serves a very useful function.

These tadpoles have just emerged from a slimy mass of frogspawn.

Various animals that live in water use slime in different ways. Hagfish and sea cucumbers use slime to escape from **predators**. The hagfish is a chief contender for the title of "World's Slimiest Creature." Lungfish use slime to stay alive when rivers and ponds dry up. Frogs use slime to protect their precious eggs. Living **organisms** in or on the surface of water, such as pond scum and red tides, are types of slime, too!

Pond slime

That gloopy green scum that floats on the surface of a pond in warm weather is actually living, breathing, bacterial slime.

Colonies of bacteria

Pond slime is not a plant, or an animal, or a type of fungus. It is made up of millions of single-celled **bacteria**. Each bacterium is a tiny ball of jelly. They join together in **colonies**, from which trail long, slimy filaments. These filaments help the slime stick together.

Microscopic size

The pond slime **organisms** are known as cyanobacteria (*SI-an-o-bak-TIR-e-a*), or sometimes blue-green algae. The shape of the **colonies** can only be seen if they are magnified.

A powerful microscope is needed to see the individual **cells**.

Oxygen makers

Cyanobacteria use the energy from sunlight to break down water molecules into the two elements they are made of, oxygen and hydrogen. They produce some of the oxygen in the air that we breathe.

Slime-ometer

Although it looks fairly disgusting, pond slime is very useful!

Overall rating: 3

The green cyanobacteria strands are woven together.

The pink specks are tiny particles of dirt.

This colony of cyanobacteria looks a bit like a sea urchin.

Slime alert!

If you touch pond slime, make sure you wash your hands afterward—some **species** of cyanobacteria are poisonous.

Slimy Stuff in Water

Slime tube

Imagine swimming along in nice warm seawater and suddenly meeting a giant slime tube that is larger than you are and pulsing with light. No, it's not some kind of strange alien—it's a pyrosome *(PIE-ro-some)*.

A zooid city

A pyrosome is a colonial marine animal that is made up of hundreds and even thousands of individuals called **zooids**. The zooids are joined together by a coating of semi-solid slime into a tube that is closed at one end.

Filter feeder

The pyrosome swims by pushing seawater out of the open end of the tube, which pushes its body forward. The tiny individual zooids, which are less than ¼ in. (6 mm) long, feed by filtering **plankton** from the water as the pyrosome moves. Pyrosomes can produce a flashing light through a process called **bioluminescence** *(BI-o-LOO-min-ess-ense)*, but scientists have not yet found out why they do this.

Adult pyrosomes can reach several yards (meters) in length and are sometimes found in shallow coastal waters.

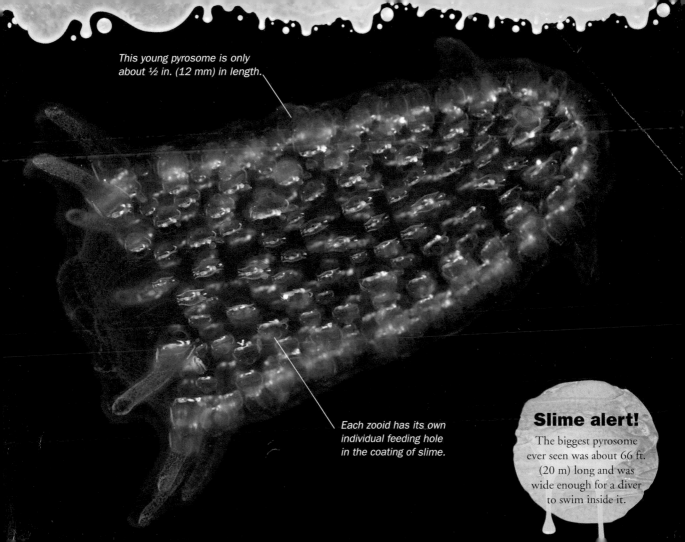

This young pyrosome is only about ½ in. (12 mm) in length.

Each zooid has its own individual feeding hole in the coating of slime.

Slime alert!

The biggest pyrosome ever seen was about 66 ft. (20 m) long and was wide enough for a diver to swim inside it.

Red tide

Seaside vacationers want bright sun, soft sand, and a clear blue sea. They do not want to paddle, surf, or swim in stinking, poisonous red slime—but that's what you get with red tide.

Slime-ometer

Red, slimy, smelly, and poisonous? What more could you want? This vile gunk scores a high rating!

Overall rating: 8

Blooming plants

Blooms of single-celled algae (the microscopic plants that naturally live in seawater) are the cause of red tides. A bloom occurs when these tiny plants suddenly multiply in number. A large bloom covers several square miles (km) of ocean surface. Problems occur if a bloom is washed onto a coast.

Concentrated poison

Some of the algae that bloom produce small amounts of poison. When washed onto a coastline, the bloom (and the poison) becomes concentrated in shallow water. These poisonous blooms often kill a large number of coastal sea creatures, such as shellfish and seabirds. Each year, many people worldwide become ill after eating shellfish that has been infected by a red tide.

Microscopic plants like this dinoflagellate (di-no-FLAJ-el-ate) are the cause of red tides.

Red tides get their name because the individual dinoflagellates are stained red by rust (iron oxide).

A severe red tide can turn a healthy stretch of coastline into a poisonous wasteland.

Slime alert!

In a red tide, there may be 30 million poison-producing dinoflagellates in every 34 fl. oz. (1 liter) of seawater.

15

Lungfish

In parts of Africa and South America, where rainfall is extremely seasonal, lungfish can survive the dry season and lack of water by burrowing into mud and covering their bodies in life-preserving slime.

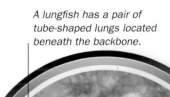

A lungfish has a pair of tube-shaped lungs located beneath the backbone.

Freshwater peril

Most fish breathe by taking oxygen from water with their **gills**, and so fish that live in freshwater are in constant danger that the water they live in will dry up. Lungfish, however, do not have this problem.

Unique feature

Lungfish have lungs and breathe air just like birds and mammals. By wriggling into mud when the water level starts to drop, they can survive months of drought safely wrapped in slime.

Slime-ometer

Slippery and goopy, but very useful and life-saving to its owner, the lungfish's slime does no harm to anyone.

Overall rating: 2

Dual purpose

The slime keeps the lungfish's skin moist in its burrow. It also forms a protective barrier against insects and **parasites** while the fish waits for the drought to end.

The lungfish is the only fish that has bones in its front fins.

When swimming, a lungfish must come to the surface to take in air through its mouth.

16

Slime alert!

In extreme circumstances, a slime-coated lungfish can survive for up to four years without water.

Horrible hagfish

The hagfish has a reputation for being the world's most disgusting sea creature, partly because of its unpleasant eating habits, but mostly because it produces the world's strongest slime.

All coiled up and slimy, the hagfish has strong defenses against enemies.

Slime eels

Hagfish live near the ocean floor, where they feed on dead and dying fish. They are often called slime eels, but hagfish are not eels. They are a very unusual type of jawless fish.

Slime-ometer

For producing vast amounts of slime and for being repulsive and unlovable, the hagfish gets a very slimy rating.

Overall rating: 9

Slimy defense

A hagfish cannot swim fast, and it has no teeth for fighting. If a **predator** attacks, it releases super-concentrated slime from its tail. Within a few seconds, this hagfish slime starts to turn the surrounding water into a thick, jellylike substance that clogs the would-be attacker's **gills**.

Sliding free

Hagfish slime is so gloopy that the animal would be in danger from its own slime were it not for a very neat trick. After defending itself and sliming an attacker, the hagfish ties its body into a knot and slides free of the thick ball of slime.

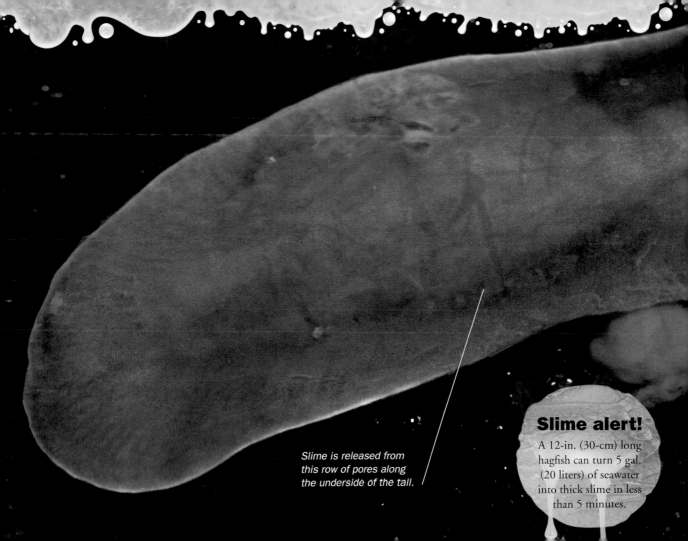

Slime is released from this row of pores along the underside of the tail.

Slime alert!

A 12-in. (30-cm) long hagfish can turn 5 gal. (20 liters) of seawater into thick slime in less than 5 minutes.

Jellyfish

Although they look extremely slimy, especially when stranded on a beach, jellyfish are in fact no slimier if you were to touch one than most other sea creatures. However, the inside of a jellyfish is mostly slime.

Newly hatched from eggs, these jellyfish are only about 1/6 in. (4 mm) wide.

Baby jellyfish are sometimes called sea lice.

Sack of slime

A jellyfish doesn't have a skeleton. Its bell-shaped body consists of two layers of skin—an outside and an inside—separated by a layer of slime. The body of a jellyfish is 97 percent water. The animal swims by using the muscles in its outer skin and pushing water out of the open end of the bell. It feeds by catching small fish with its stinging tentacles.

Slime-powered stingers

The tentacles of an adult jellyfish can reach 130 ft. (40 m) in length, and each tentacle is lined with stinging **cells**. Inside each cell is a coiled stinger, a miniature hosepipe tipped with a poisoned spike. When a tentacle touches a fish, slime is forced into the sting, which uncoils at great speed and injects poison into the unlucky victim. The tentacle then withdraws, pulling the fish into the jellyfish's mouth, which is located at the center of its underside.

Slime-ometer

With an ultra-slimy appearance and an inside full of goop, the jelly scores well.

Overall rating: 7

Slime alert!

The largest jellyfish grow
to more than 8 ft. (2.5 m)
in diameter. Fortunately,
these larger jellyfish live
in polar waters.

Sea cucumber

Sea cucumbers are soft, slow, slimy animals that are often found in large numbers on the seabed. Although they look very different, these boneless creatures are closely related to spiny, hard-shelled sea urchins.

Slime-ometer

These slimy critters may not produce tons of the slimy stuff, but what they do produce is sticky, slimy, and some of it is poisonous!

Overall rating: 5

A sticky end

Most sea cucumbers use their gooey slime as an aid to feeding, but those **species** that live in a coral reef also use it for defense. When a sea cucumber is threatened by a predator, it sends out long, sticky, poisonous strands of slime from its rear end that fatally trap all but the largest attackers.

Slimy scavengers

Sea cucumbers are scavengers—they feed on decaying plant and animal material that sinks to the seafloor. As they crawl on tiny tube feet, they gather particles of food with their slimy tentacles.

The feeding tentacles that surround the mouth are tube feet with feathery tips.

The small size of the mouth means that a sea cucumber eats only the tiniest food particles.

The tips of the tentacles are coated with sticky slime to help catch hold of food particles.

Slime alert!

Some tiny crabs and fish are immune to the sea cucumber's poisonous slime and make their home inside its digestive system.

Sea slug

In the same way that slugs slither around on land, sea slugs wriggle around beneath the sea. In contrast to their land-living relatives that are usually gray or brown, sea slugs are extremely colorful.

Slime-ometer

With a layer of gunk to keep it protected, the sea slug keeps itself and its slimy coating out of the way, beneath the sea.

Overall rating: 2

Salt barrier

On land, slugs need a coating of slime to prevent the air from drying out their delicate skin. With sea slugs, the layer of slime helps the skin maintain a barrier between the salty seawater and the water inside their bodies, which is a lot less salty. Sea slugs also need **gills** to take oxygen from the water. In some **species**, the gills form long feathery strands that trail from the back and sides.

Tiny pores in the animal's skin release slime that forms an almost invisible coating.

Feathery gills take dissolved oxygen from the water.

Colorful killers

Some sea slugs feed on marine plants, but many of them are **predators**. Most live on the ocean floor, where some **species** hunt sea snails. Others nibble at the tentacles of sea anemones, or specialize in eating sponges. A few sea slugs stay just beneath the surface of the sea and feed on drifting jellyfish.

Slime alert!

When threatened, many sea slugs can release a cloud of red or purple fluid to confuse and distract an attacker.

Sea hare

If you walk down a beach at low tide, you'll probably see lots of wet seaweed. Look more closely and you might see shiny slime trails crisscrossing the seaweed—a sign that sea hares have been feeding.

Camouflage

The sea hare is a type of plant-eating sea slug that lives in shallow coastal waters. Unlike their colorful and flesh-eating cousins, sea hares are usually the same greeny-brown color as the seaweed they eat. This camouflages them—helps them blend into the background—to avoid being spotted by hungry **predators**.

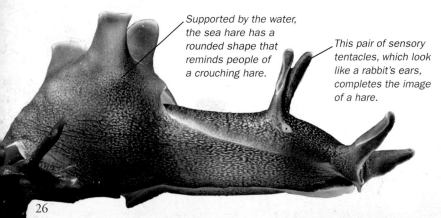

Supported by the water, the sea hare has a rounded shape that reminds people of a crouching hare.

This pair of sensory tentacles, which look like a rabbit's ears, completes the image of a hare.

Slime-ometer

Do you feel like running your hands through a bunch of wet seaweed? If so, you are likely to touch a slimy sea hare trail or two!

Overall rating: 3

Flapping escape

Some **species** of sea hare have an additional means of avoiding predators—they can flap their way out of trouble. These animals have a wide flap of skin called a parapodium (*PAR-a-PO-dee-um*), which extends from each side of the foot. Normally these parapodia are curled up against the creature's sides. But by releasing these flaps like a pair of wings, the sea hare can swim away with a rippling motion.

Slime alert!

The California black sea hare grows much bigger than any land slug and can weigh more than 4 lbs. (2 kg).

Frogspawn

Each year in spring, clumps of slimy, colorless jelly can be found in ponds and slow-moving streams all over the world. Floating just below the surface, or attached to underwater plants, this gunk is called frogspawn.

Slime-ometer

Although it is not smelly, this jellylike frogspawn is certainly gloopy, gunky, sticky, and slimy, and there's so much of it!

Overall rating: 7

Masses of eggs

These clumps of jelly are the eggs of frogs and toads. Unlike the eggs of birds and reptiles, these soft, slimy eggs do not have an outer shell.

Protective slime

Frogs and toads are **amphibians**—animals that spend much of their time in water but can also live on land. They do not have hair, feathers, or scales to protect their skin. Instead, they have a slimy covering that keeps their skin nice and moist when they are on land.

The tadpoles feed on the jelly inside the egg for about a week before they hatch.

The eggs are sticky and clump together in a big, gloopy, slimy mass.

At the center of each jelly-filled egg is a tiny tadpole (the young form of a frog or toad).

Slime alert!

In spring, in places where
there are few ponds but
plenty of frogs or toads,
a small pond can turn
into one big mass of
slimy jelly.

29

Slimy Stuff on Land

Slime is an even more useful substance on dry land, where it is often used as a life-preserving substitute for water. Slime can also be used by creatures as a weapon to capture food and kill enemies.

Many land animals, such as **amphibians** (frogs, toads, and newts) and **mollusks** (soft-bodied creatures that sometimes have a shell,

This insect, a froghopper nymph, hides beneath slimy bubbles for protection.

for example, slugs and snails), are dependent on slime. They must keep their bodies covered in a layer of slime to prevent their skin from drying out. Cane toads produce a form of poisonous slime. Some frogs and all froghoppers create a special frothy slime to protect their vulnerable young. Velvet worms and some glowworms use especially sticky slime to trap other animals for food. But animals are not the only producers of slime on land—some plants and fungi also make slime.

31

Poison arrow frog

Being covered in slime is all part of being a good parent for this South American male poison arrow frog. The slime keeps a pair of tadpoles nice and moist while they are carried piggyback to a new home.

Slime-ometer

Slime-covered and with extra goop oozing out, the poison arrow frog scores points for having poisonous slime, too.

Overall rating: 7

Tree life

Frogs that live in ponds can leave their tadpoles to fend for themselves, but there are few ponds in the South American rainforest. The poison arrow frog is a tree frog and it makes do with the tiny pools of water that collect at the center of some plants. When its tadpoles have outgrown a pool, the male carries them to a bigger pool.

Slime oozes out of pores in the frog's skin.

As well as breathing air through lungs, some adult amphibians can also absorb oxygen through their skin, as long as it is kept moist.

Slimy skin

Frogs are **amphibians**, and like all other amphibians, they have very slimy skin. When it is time to move its young, the poison arrow frog produces extra slime to coat the tadpoles. The slime is poisonous to all other animals.

Slime alert!

Poison arrow frogs do not
need camouflage to keep
them safe—their bright
color is a warning:
"Do Not Eat!"

Foam-nest frog

When walking through a tropical rainforest, you never know what is going to drip down and fall onto your head. If you are very unlucky, it will be a great big drop of slimy, wriggling tadpoles.

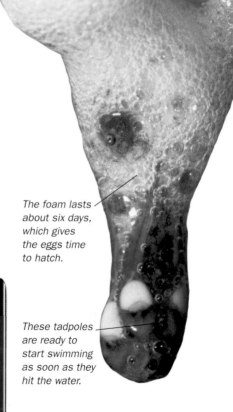

Bubble builder

Foam-nest frogs do not lay their eggs in ponds. Instead, they prefer to make a nest high in the trees above a pond or river. They choose a curled-over leaf and then froth up their slime by blowing bubbles into it until they have made a ball of slimy foam. The eggs are laid in the middle of the nest and then are left to fend for themselves.

Fall to freedom

After the eggs hatch, the foam keeps the tadpoles moist and

discourages **predators**, such as spiders, but the tadpoles are trapped in the treetops. As they grow in size, their weight causes the leaf to bend and the tadpoles drip down into the water below.

Slime-ometer

Slimy tadpoles dripping down your neck! Yuck and double yuck—this frog gets a high score.

Overall rating: 8

The foam lasts about six days, which gives the eggs time to hatch.

These tadpoles are ready to start swimming as soon as they hit the water.

Female foam-nest frogs sometimes work together to build a shared nest.

34

Slime alert!

The average nest built by these frogs contains about 800 eggs and more than 17 fl. oz. (0.5 liters) of slimy foam.

California newt

This North American **amphibian** spends most of its life out of water. A coating of slime prevents its skin from drying out. This slime also means that the California newt has little to fear from **predators**.

Shy and slimy

During the breeding season, California newts gather to lay eggs in slow-moving streams. The rest of the year, they keep cool under rocks or fallen trees. Predators have learned not to hunt for these newts because their slime is a deadly poison.

Slime-ometer

With a very slimy coating that is ultra-deadly to attackers, the California newt scores high.

Overall rating: 8

Paralyzing poison

This newt's slime contains a chemical called tetrodotoxin *(TE-trod-o-TOX-in)*, which is more than a hundred times more powerful than cyanide. It is poisonous, and there is no known remedy. It attacks the nervous system and paralyzes muscles. Unable to breathe, the victim dies quickly from lack of oxygen. This newt doesn't have poison-producing glands. Scientists believe it develops the poison by eating **bacteria**.

A fully-grown California newt measures about 6 in. (16 cm) in length.

Slime alert!

About 0.035 oz. (1 g) of tetrodotoxin in California newt slime is enough to kill about 2,000 adult humans.

Water-holding frog

In the vast semi-deserts of the Australian outback, there is one animal—the water-holding frog—that has found a slimy solution to the problem of surviving for long periods without rainfall and water.

Sudden downpours

Rainfall is very unpredictable in the outback. There can be no rain for more than a year, and then a sudden torrential downpour can turn the ground into a sea of mud. When this happens, the water-holding frog takes on as much water as its body can hold.

Slime-ometer

For keeping its slime-covered body buried and out of sight, the water-holding frog scores low.

Overall rating: 1

Cocoon of slime

While the ground is still soft and damp, the frog burrows down to a depth of about 30 in. (80 cm). The coating of slime on its body hardens into a waterproof cocoon (protective covering), and the frog simply waits for the next rainfall. The native inhabitants of Australia know all about the frog's technique, and it was they who gave the animal its popular name. They learned how to dig up these frogs and gently squeeze out the water for a refreshing drink.

The cocoon of hardened slime covers the whole body while the frog is in its burrow.

A cocooned frog can survive for more than two years without rain.

Slime alert!

Surprisingly, the water squeezed out from one of these frogs is completely fresh and safe to drink.

Cane toad

The cane toad is a hulking brute of an **amphibian** that oozes a milky-white and highly poisonous slime from special glands on its neck. This large toad is also a ravenous hunter that swallows its **prey** whole.

Slime-ometer

Large, ugly, and oozing goopy drops of poisonous slime, the cane toad is not just slimy, it's dangerous!

Overall rating: 8

The milky-white droplets are nearly pure poison.

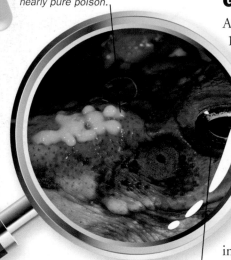
Parotid glands located behind the eyes produce highly dangerous slime.

Giant toad

A fully grown cane toad is about 12 in. (30 cm) long and weighs more than 4 lbs. (2 kg). It hunts and eats a variety of small animals, including mice, small birds, lizards, frogs, and large numbers of **invertebrates**. Originally from Central America, the cane toad gets its name because it was introduced to other countries to control pests in fields of sugar cane. Unfortunately, it has itself now become a pest.

Poisonous slime

The main problem with the cane toad, apart from its habit of eating wildlife and domestic pets, is the poisonous slime produced by the adult toads. This slime contains substances called bufotoxins *(BU-fo-TOX-ins)*. These are highly poisonous to many animals, but not to the toads themselves.

Slime alert!

Anyone who thinks a nice fat cane toad would make a tasty meal had better think again. People have died after eating this animal.

Velvet worm

At night in the rainforest, velvet worms emerge from under rotting logs to search for food. Slowly and silently they creep up on their unsuspecting **prey**, which they trap in a sticky net of slime.

Slime-ometer

It creeps, it crawls, and it squirts out super-sticky gluelike slime—the velvet worm is a slime-squirting attacker.

Overall rating: 7

A velvet worm has tiny, hard claws at the tip of each leg.

Glue guns

A velvet worm has a pair of sensory tentacles at the front of its head for detecting **prey**. Just behind the tentacles it has a pair of "glue guns" that squirt jets of sticky slime onto its prey. The slime dries quickly and paralyzes the victim so that the velvet worm can feed at its leisure.

Slime glands in the creature's head make up about 10 percent of its body weight.

Tropical terrors

Velvet worms are about 5 in. (12 cm) long. They are found throughout the tropical regions, and in some cooler woodlands. They might look like caterpillars, but velvet worms are fully grown adults that make good use of their handy slime.

These tentacles combine the senses of taste, smell, and touch, which is ideal for an animal that hunts at night.

Slime alert!

After hunting, the velvet worm eats any unused hardened slime and recycles it to use next time.

Slime light

In caves and gloomy forests in New Zealand, tiny lights glow in the darkness. Flying insects attracted by these lights soon find themselves entangled in long threads coated with sticky slime.

Fishing lines

The grublike **larvae** of small insects known as fungus gnats produce these glowing lights as a lure for their "fishing lines." After hatching, these larvae, or glowworms, cling to the roof of a cave or under the branches of a tree.

Adult fungus gnats cannot feed—their only purpose is to reproduce.

Eggs laid by the female will hatch into flesh-eating larvae.

Slime-ometer

With slime-coated threads dangling down, ready to trap insects, the glowworm is a clever little slime producer.

Overall rating: 5

Chemical glow

Once attached to a roof or branch, each **larva** then spins threads of silk that dangle down beneath it to create the "fishing lines." Poisonous slime from the larva's body slides down the threads to form a series of sticky droplets. When its fishing line is complete, the larva produces a glowing light with chemicals stored in its abdomen. Any insect that flies into the thread becomes stuck in the droplets of slime. The larva can then reel in its catch to eat it.

Slime alert!

Fungus gnat larvae can reel in their slime-trapped **prey** at a rate of about ½ in. (10 mm) every five seconds.

Snail

Most of us have come across snail slime at some point. Snails leave a telltale trail of glistening slime behind them wherever they travel—on leaves, rocks, walls, paths, plants, and windows.

Slime coated

Snails are found in all but the coldest parts of the world. A snail's body is coated with a thin layer of slime, and it needs this slime to help it move.

a coating of slime. The slime also helps it climb vertical surfaces, and even walk upside down.

Big foot

A snail has no legs—the underside of its body is one big foot. The animal slithers along with

Slime-ometer

Snails get everywhere! For having slime-producing glands in their feet and leaving their goop all over the place, the snail scores well.

Overall rating: 5

In dry conditions, a snail can withdraw into its shell and seal the opening with dried slime.

Dried snail slime often looks silvery in sunlight.

Slime alert!

In Africa, the world's largest snails grow to be almost 16 in. (40 cm) in length and weigh more than 2 lbs. (1 kg).

47

Banana slug

There aren't any bananas in the warm rainforest along the northwest coast of the United States. However, there is an abundance of big, fat, slimy, yellow banana slugs.

Snails without shells

Slugs are closely related to snails and are sometimes described as "snails without shells." In fact, some slugs have small shells, but none have a spiral shell to withdraw into like snails. Slugs must use even more slime to keep their bodies moist, and the banana slug is no slimy exception.

Slimy descent

Banana slugs that climb to the end of a branch have a neat trick for getting back down. They let their bodies fall off the branch until they are only attached by a "rope" made of their thick slime. By producing more slime, the slugs can lengthen the rope and lower themselves to the ground. Their big, fat, yellow bodies, often with black spots, look just like bananas hanging down from the trees.

Slime-ometer

There are few things more disgusting than walking through a forest and getting slapped in the face by a dangling banana slug.

Overall rating: 8

Slugs have two pairs of tentacles on their heads. The longer pair of tentacles is sensitive to light, while the other pair is used to detect tastes and scents.

Slugs and snails feed by rubbing away at vegetation with a rough tonguelike organ located under their heads.

Slime alert!

Growing to about 10 in. (25 cm) in length, the Pacific banana slug is the world's second largest land-living slug.

Slime mold beetle

Imagine living on a diet of slime—slime for breakfast, slime for lunch, and more slime for supper. If this doesn't appeal to you, then consider the life of a slime mold beetle, which just eats slime.

Shiny casing

A slime mold beetle is not a slimy creature. Like other beetles, it has a hard shiny casing called an exoskeleton and it walks on six jointed legs. There is nothing slimy about its appearance, but it has a very slimy appetite. Other beetles eat a wide variety of foods. Some hunt other insects, and some are plant-eaters. Slime mold beetles, however, eat nothing but living slime.

Slime-ometer

Despite having eating habits that reveal its taste for slime, the slime mold beetle is a slime-free animal and scores low.

Overall rating: 2

Strange food

These tiny beetles, no more than ⅙ in. (4 mm) in length, are found in all parts of the world scuttling around fallen trees on forest floors. They feed on slime molds, which are very strange **organisms** that "grow"

The beetle slices off pieces of slime mold with its sharp mandibles (biting mouthparts).

on dead plants. Slime molds are some of the strangest and most puzzling of all living things.

Slime alert!

The largest slime molds can extend over several square yards (meters), but only as a very thin layer.

Slimy Stuff on Land
Froghopper

Running your fingers through the plants in a meadow can be a very pleasant experience—until you find a glob of slimy wet bubbles that looks like spit.

Slime-ometer

Froghopper froth is wet and slimy, and there is lots of it around in the summer, but it's not too bad unless you run your hands through it.

Overall rating: 3

Whose spit?

So what sort of animal is doing all this spitting? In fact, it is not spit. That slimy wetness on your fingers is insect froth produced by froghoppers, which are also known as spittlebugs.

As the froth turns back into a liquid, it drips down onto the ground.

Sap suckers

Froghoppers are small insects about ½ in. (10 mm) long. Young froghoppers, called nymphs, cling to plant stems and suck out the sap (the fluid found inside the plant). The nymphs use some of the liquid sap to produce a nasty-tasting froth that surrounds their bodies. This froth protects them from **predators** and also keeps the nymphs warm during cold nights.

Froghoppers belong to a group of insects whose nymphs look like miniature adults instead of grublike larvae.

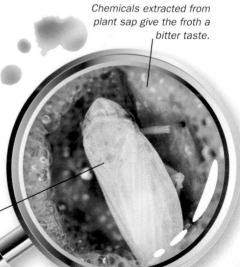

Chemicals extracted from plant sap give the froth a bitter taste.

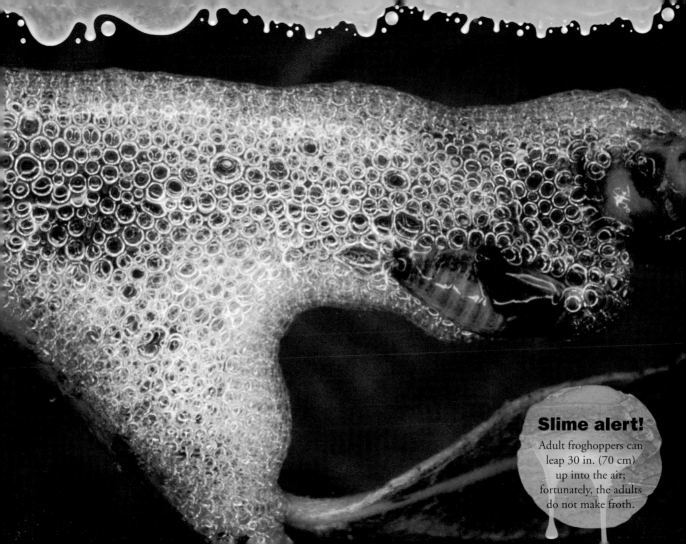

Slime alert!

Adult froghoppers can
leap 30 in. (70 cm)
up into the air;
fortunately, the adults
do not make froth.

Starfish stinkhorn

There's slime, there's smelly slime, and then there's the utterly revolting and foul-smelling slime produced by the starfish stinkhorn fungus. The stench is somewhere between sewage and rotting meat.

Slime-ometer

The starfish stinkhorn scores high for sliminess and earns maximum bonus points for its disgusting smell. Yuck!

Overall rating: 10

Slimy traveler

The starfish stinkhorn, which is also known as the sea anemone fungus, is about the size of a child's hand. Originally from Australia, it has spread to the islands of the Pacific Ocean and is now common in Hawaii.

Attractive slime

The stinkhorn starts as a small egg-shaped sac that opens out to reveal bright red arms in a starfish shape. The slime, which is called gleba, oozes out at the base of the arms to attract flies.

Flies love the smell of rotting meat from the glistening brown slime.

*The slime contains thousands of tiny **spores**—each one can grow to make a new stinkhorn.*

The gleba must taste as good as it looks—to flies at least, because they gulp down as much as they can, eating the spores at the same time.

When a fly leaves its droppings elsewhere, it spreads the spores, new stinkhorns grow, and the slimy cycle continues.

Slime alert!

The starfish stinkhorn is still rare in North America, but its **spores** are spreading the stinky slime.

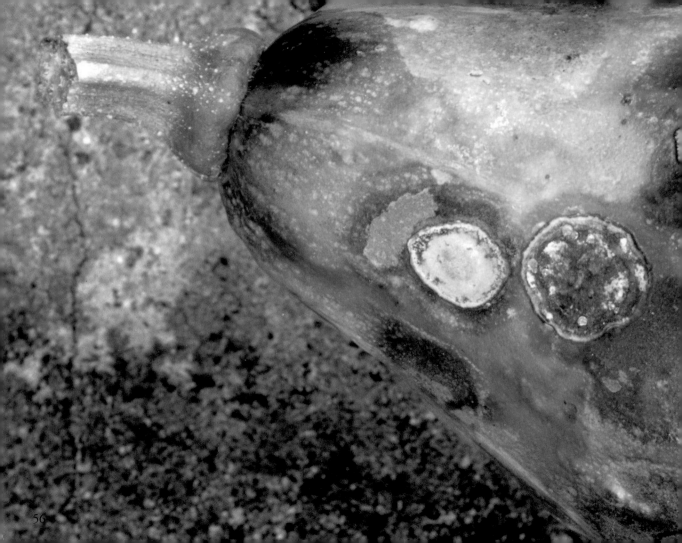

Other Slimy Stuff

Slime can look, feel, and smell disgusting, and can make you feel quite ill to think about. But slime is part of life, and even our own bodies are continually producing vast amounts of it.

We coat our food in a thin layer of slime called saliva before we swallow it, and a different sort of slime protects the delicate inner surfaces of our lungs. When we are ill, this slime becomes infected with **bacteria** and turns into an utterly vile substance known as phlegm *(flem)*. Some slime is associated with decay and **decomposition**, the process of rotting. Decomposition often results in a gloopy, slimy mess—decomposing, rotting vegetables is a slimy example. Some other slime is not yet fully understood. For scientists, the humble slime molds are some of the most interesting **organisms** on Earth.

Patches of **yeast** and mold, which are types of fungi, mark the surface of a decomposing squash.

Saliva

Saliva is a very useful sort of slime. It helps us chew and swallow our food. Our own saliva is perfectly safe, but what about the saliva of other animals?

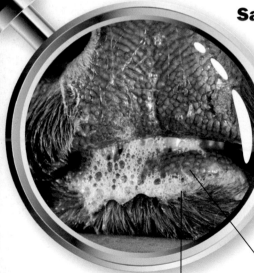

Saliva may collect bacteria from rotting food between teeth.

Salivary glands

Saliva is produced by salivary glands located inside your head around the mouth. Saliva makes our food slippery and easy to swallow. It helps in other ways as well. Saliva contains enzymes *(EN-zimes)*, substances that help to break down food so that your body can convert it into energy.

Mammals, like this cow, have three pairs of salivary glands situated around the mouth.

Deadly slime

Some animals, such as spiders, inject saliva into the bodies of their victims. The enzymes contained in their saliva break down body tissues (materials that make up the body) into a liquid that can be slurped up like soup. Some snakes have highly poisonous saliva that is used to kill their **prey**.

Slime-ometer

Most animals have saliva, but some of it is pretty nasty and drips, froths, foams, or dribbles out of the mouth.

Overall rating: 6

The saliva of the Komodo dragon contains dangerous bacteria that will infect any creature that it bites.

Slime alert!

Large amounts of saliva
can often be a sign of ill
health, although different
animals produce
different amounts.

Other Slimy Stuff

Phlegm

This is by far the most disgusting and unpleasant type of slime produced by the human body. There is no such thing as healthy phlegm—all phlegm is unhealthy and a sign of a problem.

Slime-ometer

Yuck! Phlegm is truly disgusting. It has to be one of the most unpleasant forms of slime.

Overall rating: 10

Reaction to attack

The **membranes** that line the inside of the windpipe and lungs produce phlegm. These membranes are kept moist with a naturally slimy substance known as mucus. When the membranes are attacked—either by dust and smoke particles or by disease-causing **bacteria** or viruses—they react by producing phlegm.

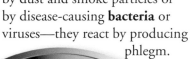

Bacteria show up as circular objects.

This sample of dried phlegm (magnified about 400 times) clearly shows yellowish fibrous strands of dried mucus.

Pink structures are fragments of the lining of the windpipe.

Garbage disposal

Phlegm is made up of mucus, dead membrane **cells**, and other things that the body considers to be garbage—particles of dust and smoke, or dead and dying **bacteria**. These give phlegm its disgusting color. When phlegm is in the lungs and windpipe, it causes a muscle reflex (a cough), and this sends the phlegm into the mouth.

Phlegm that has been mixed with saliva and spat out of the mouth is called sputum (SPEW-tum).

Slime alert!

The phlegm of people infested with hookworms may contain the **larvae** of these **parasites**.

61

Sundew plant

A thirsty insect sees sparkling droplets of water on a plant and settles down for a drink. But the sparkling droplets are sticky slime—the hapless insect is stuck and the plant is hungry.

Diet supplement

Sundew plants grow on marshy ground that contains few minerals and **nutrients**. The plants get around this problem by catching insects and taking minerals and nutrients from their bodies. The plant's leaves are covered with small tendrils tipped with droplets of a very sticky substance called mucilage (*MU-si-lij*).

Dissolving slime

After the sticky tendrils have trapped an insect, they slowly curl inward and completely surround it. The tendrils then release a thin slime that contains chemicals to dissolve the insect's body. The insect is turned into a "soup" that the plant absorbs through the surface of its leaves.

The tendrils are sensitive to the slightest touch.

The more the insect struggles, the tighter the tendrils curl.

Slime-ometer

Stay clear if you are an insect, but don't worry if you are a human—the sundew's sticky slime is harmless to humans.

Overall rating: 2

Slime alert!

In one **species** of sundew, the tendrils can close around an insect in less than one-tenth of a second.

Other Slimy Stuff

Slime flux

A tree may appear to be completely healthy when viewed from a distance. However, a closer view might reveal a problem and show that it is leaking a frothy, slimy, and foul-smelling substance called slime flux.

Slime-ometer

Slimy and smelly, slime flux is pretty nasty if you are a tree, but otherwise it's not too bad.

Overall rating: 3

Bacterial infection

Some trees have a condition known as bacterial wetwood. They might suffer a physical wound, perhaps by a branch being broken, and a **bacterium** enters the wound. As the bacterium spreads and multiplies inside the tree, it causes changes to the sap that bubbles out through the bark. This altered sap attracts other bacteria and molds that combine to produce the slime flux. The sap also attracts insects and birds. These insects might cause further damage to the tree.

Widespread problem

Many common forest and garden tree **species** suffer from slime flux, including oak, elm, beech, birch, maple, hickory, and cherry. Little can be done to prevent the infection because the bacteria that cause it are found in most kinds of soil.

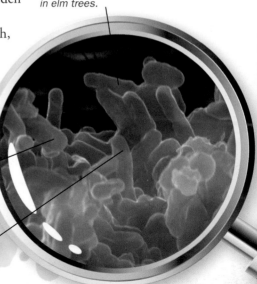

The bacterium Enterobacter cloacae causes slime flux in elm trees.

This image of bacteria has been magnified 5,000 times.

The individual bacterium have a distinctive rod shape.

64

Slime alert!

Slime flux oozing from a tree trunk might even attract clusters of maggots.

Decomposing vegetables

Fresh vegetables are crisp and crunchy, and good to eat. How about old vegetables—the ones that are soft and have a slimy center? They are not quite so good. Welcome to the world of the decomposers.

Tiny dots of decomposer **yeast** are growing on a slice of pumpkin.

The hardcoated seeds are much more resistant to decomposers than the pulpy flesh.

Liquified food

Decomposers are the **bacteria**, molds, **yeasts**, and other **microorganisms** that specialize in feeding on dead plants and animals. These decomposers thrive in warm, wet conditions. Storing food in cool, dry conditions can slow down the work of the decomposers, but it cannot stop them completely.

Recycling

With fruit and vegetables, the process of **decomposition** begins as soon as they are separated from the living plant. The internal structure of their **cells** starts to break down, and they become vulnerable to decomposers. If the outer skin is cut or broken, the process of decomposition is sped up. Decomposition is a very efficient means of recycling **nutrients**. In the kitchen, however, it smells and looks very unpleasant.

Slime-ometer

Decomposing vegetables for lunch? Yuck! Some of the most colorful slime is produced by old vegetables.

Overall rating: 6

Slime alert!

Pelting criminals
with decomposing
vegetables was a popular
punishment during the
Middle Ages.

Jelly fungus

In the woods in damp weather, you could see glistening blobs of slime on fallen branches. They might not look alive, but these blobs are actually a type of living jelly fungus.

Consuming the dead

Fungi grow by taking **nutrients** from dead and decaying plants. Some **species** also grow on living trees. Most of the time, a fungus consists of thin fibers hidden below ground or in a fallen log. The parts of the fungus that we can see, such as jelly fungi and toadstools, are **fruiting bodies** that produce **spores** so the fungus can spread.

Witch's butter

In dry weather, a jelly fungus shrinks and dries into a hard lump. In damp conditions, it expands into a jellylike mass. People used to call these blobs "witch's butter" because they have such an unpleasant taste.

Some species look more like slimy flowers than fungi.

The underside of the jelly tongue fungus is covered with tiny, soft spines.

The tip of each spine releases microscopic spores into the air.

Slime-ometer

The slimy, glistening blobs of jelly fungus wouldn't taste good, but they are not harmful.
Overall rating: 4

Slime alert!
Some jelly fungi grow in a branching shape like coral, while others look more like damp seaweed.

Other Slimy Stuff
Lattice stinkhorn

It may look like a delicious piece of juicy tropical fruit drizzled with chocolate sauce, but looks can be very deceiving—unless you happen to be a fly. That lovely sauce is a special fly-attracting slime.

Red baskets

The lattice stinkhorn is a fungus that produces small, red, basket-shaped **fruiting bodies** about 2 in. (5 cm) in diameter. As the fruiting bodies ripen, these "baskets" open and a greenish-brown slime oozes onto the inner surfaces. This slime, which is known as gleba *(GLEE-ba)*, contains millions of microscopic **spores**. Each one of these tiny spores can grow into another lattice stinkhorn.

Slime-ometer

Very slimy, very smelly, and covered with buzzing flies—so it's no surprise that the lattice stinkhorn scores high. Yuck!

Overall rating: 9

This fruiting body is bursting out of its protective sheath and revealing its basket-shaped structure.

Spore-bearing slime (gleba) produced in these hollows will stick to the legs of flies and other insect visitors.

Disgusting stench

The lattice stinkhorn deserves its name. The gleba has a disgusting smell, somewhere between sewers and rotting meat. Humans steer well clear when walking in the forest because the smell will stick to shoes for days. But flies and other insects love to stomp around in the slime, and that is how the fungus is spread.

Slime alert!

The lattice stinkhorn is native to Europe but spread to North America in soil around plants shipped across the Atlantic Ocean.

Creeping slime

If you examine a forest floor with a magnifying glass, you may discover what looks like a slug creeping over the fallen leaves. This "slug" is an organized group of **amoebas** (single-celled **organisms**).

This slime mold has crawled to the top of a tree stump, leaving a trail of stringy slime behind it.

Mass emigration

A slime mold consists of many thousands of single-celled amoebas *(a-MEE-bas)* that have learned to stick together. When conditions are good, slime molds exist as a thin layer spread out over the ground. But if conditions become unfavorable, the slime mold forms itself into a sluglike shape and crawls away to find a better location.

Coordinated action

Although it looks and moves like a larger, multi-celled animal, the slime mold "slug" is still a collection of individuals. Scientists do not yet fully understand how all these individuals coordinate their movements. And how do they decide in which direction to travel? Slime is full of secrets just waiting to be discovered.

Slime-ometer

Creeping, crawling, shape-changing, and showing signs of high intelligence? This creepy slime mold deserves a good slimy rating.

Overall rating: 7

Slime alert!
Fortunately for us, slime mold "slugs" are less than ¼ in. (6 mm) in length.

Living snot mold

A slime mold doesn't make slime, it is slime—and it is sometimes known as "living snot." This slime mold consists of extremely small **organisms** that have joined together, and it may spread over several square yards.

Slime-ometer

Living snot? What a great and fitting name for this gooey stuff, which doesn't make slime, but actually is slime! Yuck!

Overall rating: 6

Living slime

Despite its name, a slime mold is not a fungus, but a bizarre type of **amoeba** that lives in **colonies**, or groups. Instead of having individual **cells** surrounded by a cell wall, the slime mold amoebas form a single, gooey blob of slime.

The stalked fruiting bodies of a slime mold fooled scientists into thinking it was a fungus.

Appropriate name

Slime molds can be found on rotting wood and plants in most warm, damp parts of the world. One **species**, the Dog Vomit slime mold, often invades yards, where it is an unattractive feature.

*The fruiting body contains microscopic **spores** that will be released into the air.*

By forming narrow tubes, the slime mold can "crawl" over surfaces.

Slime alert!

Slime molds are "intelligent," experiments have shown that they can find the shortest way through a maze to reach food.

Glossary

Amoeba
A single-celled organism that looks like a microscopic blob of jelly.

Amphibian
A cold-blooded animal with a backbone and delicate skin that is protected by a layer of slime.

Bacteria (singular: bacterium)
A group of single-celled organisms that can live in almost every environment; bacteria do not have nuclei like other cells.

Bioluminescence
Chemical light produced by some animals, especially certain species of insect and fish.

Cell
The basic building-block from which all living things are made. The human body is made up of about 100 trillion cells.

Colony
In the science of living things, a colony is a group of individual organisms that are physically connected to each other.

Decomposer
Any of the microorganisms that assist in the process of decomposition.

Decomposition
The process by which dead organisms are broken down and recycled by nature.

Fruiting body
The visible part of a fungus that contains spores.

Gill
An organ used by animals that live in water to take dissolved oxygen from water.

Invertebrate
An animal that does not have a backbone.

Larva (plural: larvae)
The immature stage in the life cycle of some animals, including many insects and sea creatures.

Membrane
A thin wall of living tissue that internally separates one part of the body from another.

Microorganism

An organism that is too small to be seen without a microscope.

Mollusk

A member of a group of invertebrate animals that includes snails, slugs, squid, and octopuses.

Nutrient

A substance obtained from the environment that is essential to the well-being of an organism.

Organism

Any living thing— such as a plant, animal, or fungus.

Parasite

An organism that lives in or on the body of another organism from which it obtains food.

Plankton

Tiny organisms, such as bacteria, and larger animals, such as jellyfish, that drift in water.

Predator

An animal that catches and eats other animals.

Prey

An animal that is eaten by another animal.

Species

A particular type of organism— all the members of a species have the same set of characteristics.

Spore

A type of seed produced by some plants and fungi.

Yeast

A type of microscopic fungus.

Zooid

One of the individual organisms that make up a colonial animal.

Index

Acknowledgments

Marshall Editions would like to thank the following for their kind permission to reproduce their images.

Key: **t** = top **b** = bottom **c** = center **r** = right **l** = left

Cover Image: FLPA/Tony Hamblin
1 Shutterstock/Jiri Heral; 2 Shutterstock/ Steffen Foerster Photography; 3 Corbis/Michael & Patricia Fogden; 5 Philip Baird/Mushroom Observer 6bl Alamy/Worldthroughthelens-medical; 6t Alamy/Peter Arnold, Inc; 6br Getty Images/Photolibrary/Michael Pitts; 7tl Shutterstock/Peter Baxter; 7br FLPA/ Cyril Ruoso; 8 Ardea/Auscape/Densey Clyne; 9 Shutterstock/Anteromite; 10 Science Photo Library/Dr Jeremy Burgess; 11 Image Quest Marine; 12 Photolibrary/OSF/Mark Conlin; 13 Nick Hobgood/Encyclopedia of Life; 14 US Geological Survey; 15 Getty Images/ Photolibrary/Michael Pitts; 16 NaturePL/Nature Production; 17 FLPA/Frank W Lane; 18 NaturePL/Brandon Cole; 19 Corbis/ Brandon D Cole; 20l Alamy/cbimages; 20c Shutterstock/Laitr Keiows; 21 Alamy/ Wildlife GmbH; 22bl FLPA/Frans Lanting; 22br & 23 Shutterstock/Nikita Tiunov; 24 -25 Shutterstock/John A Anderson; 26 NaturePL/Christophe Courteau; 27 Photolibrary/WaterFrame/

Underwater Images/Wolfgang Poelzer; 28cl Shutterstock; 28br Shutterstock/Peter Baxter; 29 Shutterstock/Gertjan Hooijer; 30-31 Shutterstock/Jip Fens; 32cl Shutterstock/ Fivespots; 32br & 32t Alamy/Martin Harvey; 33 Corbis/Michael & Patricia Fogden; 34 Corbis/Michael & Patricia Fogden; 35 Photolibrary/Fotosearch; 36-37 Alamy/ Design Pics Inc; 38-39 Ardea/D Parer & E Parer-Cook; 40l NaturePL/Jurgen Freund; 40r Shutterstock/Johan Larson; 41 Shutterstock/ Jason Mintzer; 42 Shutterstock/Dr Morley Read; 43 NaturePL/John Downer; Productions/ Rod Clarke; 44 Springbrook Research Centre, Queensland, Australia; 45 FLPA/Michael & Patricia Fogden; 46bl Shutterstock/Jiri Hera; 46bc FLPA/Maurice Nimmo; 46cr Shutterstock/ Ivostar; 47 Alamy/Oliver Smart; 48l Shutterstock/Steffen Foerster Photography; 48r Shutterstock/Dee Golden; 49 Nathan deBruyn/Eon Photography; 50-52 Christoph Benisch; 52l Science Photo Library/Dr Morley Read; 52br Science Photo Library/Stephen J Krasemann; 53 Science Photo Library/Dr John

Brackenbury; 54 Shutterstock/Noam Armonn; 54 Shutterstock/Le Do; 55 Corbis/Michael & Patricia Fogden; 56-57 Science Photo Library/ Astrid & Hanns-Frieder Michler; 58 Alamy/Bison; 59 FLPA/Minden Pictures/ Cyril Ruoso; 60 Science Photo Library/SCIMAT; 61 Alamy/Alamy/Worldthroughthelens-medical; 62 FLPA/Minden Pictures/Jim Brandenburg; 63 Corbis/Frans Lanting; 64 Science Photo Library/Eye Of Science; 65 USDA/Forest Service/Forestry Images/Joseph O'Brien; 66 Science Photo Library/Dr Jeremy Burgess; 67 Shutterstock/Nikita Tiunov; 68bl Alamy/ Peter Arnold Inc; 68tr Science Photo Library/ Vaughan Fleming; 69 Alamy/Peter Arnold, Inc; 70 Alan Rockefeller/Musroom Observer; 71 Philip Baird/Mushroom Observer; 72 FLPA/Richard Becker; 73 FLPA/Minden Pictures/Sterre Delemarre; 74 Kim Fleming/ Flickr/Myriorama; 75 FLPA/Richard Becker; 76 Photolibrary/David M Dennis; 77 Getty Images/National Geographic Creative/ Stephen Sharnoff; 78 Shutterstock/Ivostar; All other images: Shutterstock.